Tennessee Heritage

McDougal Littell
A DIVISION OF HOUGHTON MIFFLIN COMPANY

Art Acknowledgements

5 Courtesy of the U.S. Geological Survey; **6** © Thinkstock Images/Jupiterimages Corporation; **7** © Bill Manning/istockphoto.com; **9** © Tim Whittaker/Shutterstock; **12** Library of Congress, Prints and Photographs Division [LC-USZ6-674]; **13** Library of Congress, Prints and Photographs Division [LC-USZ62-116498]; **16** Library of Congress, Prints and Photographs Division [LC-USZ62-37338]; **16** © Harvey Hessler/Shutterstock; **20** *Andrew Jackson* (about 1857), Thomas Sully. Oil on canvas, mounted on board, 29.25" x 24.25". U.S. Senate Collection (Cat. No. 32.00018.000); Library of Congress, Prints and Photographs Division [LC-DIG-ppmsca-09599]; **21** Library of Congress, Prints and Photographs Division [LC-USZ62-93521]; **22** Library of Congress, Prints and Photographs Division [LC-USZ62-1491]; **24** Library of Congress, Prints and Photographs Division [LC-USZ62-5092]; Library of Congress, Prints and Photographs Division [LC-USZC4-1910; **26** Library of Congress, Prints and Photographs Division [LC-USZ62-13017]; **27** Library of Congress, Prints and Photographs Division [LC-USZ62-100552]; **28** Ida B. Wells. Library of Congress, Prints and Photographs Division [LC-USZ62-107756]; **30** Library of Congress, Prints and Photographs Division [LC-DIG-ggbain-29128]; **31** Library of Congress, Prints and Photographs Division [LC-DIG-ggbain-37226]; **32** © Bettmann/Corbis; **33** Diagram of TVA Water Control System. Library of Congress, Prints and Photographs Division [LC-USW33-015690-ZC]; **36** *USS Shaw* explodes during the Japanese raid on Pearl Harbor, December 7, 1941. National Archives; **37** Library of Congress, Prints and Photographs Division [LC-USZ62-36452]; **37** Library of Congress, Prints and Photographs Division [LC-DIG-ggbain-33615]; **39** National Archives; **44** © KennStilger47/Shutterstock; **48** © Thinkstock Images/Jupiterimages Corporation; **48** Public Domain; **49** Bettmann/Corbis; **50** © Jami Garrison/istockphoto.com; **51** GeoNova LLC **52** Courtesy of the Tennessee Department of State; **53** © Robin Holden, Sr./Shutterstock; **54** © fotosearch.com; **55** © Jupiterimages Corporation.

ISBN-10: 0-547-11797-3

ISBN-13: 978-0-547-11797-3

1 2 3 4 5 6 7 8 9 – DSHV – 10 09 08 07

Table of Contents
Tennessee Heritage

Timeline of Tennessee History

15000 B.C. to 5000 B.C.	Paleo Indians occupied the area.
6000 B.C. to 1000 B.C.	Archaic Indians created mussel shell mounds along the Cumberland River.
1000 B.C. to 1100 A.D.	Woodland Indians, known for their mound building, occupied the area.
1100 A.D. to 1600 A.D.	Mississippian Indians occupied the area.
1541	Hernando de Soto, an early Spanish explorer, visited the Tennessee area. He went as far north as Chattanooga and claimed the area was under Spanish possession.
1600s	Cherokee Indians occupied east Tennessee. Creek Indians lived along the Tennessee River and in south middle Tennessee. Chickasaws inhabited west Tennessee along the Mississippi River.
1673	James Needham was sent by a Virginia trader to scout trade with the Cherokee Indians.
1682	Shawnees tried to permanently settle in Tennessee.
1715	The last Shawnees were driven out by Chickasaw and Cherokee attacks.
1770s	Four different communities were established in northeastern Tennessee—on the Watauga River, the North Holston, the Nolichucky, and in Carter's Valley.
1779–1780	During the winter and spring, three hundred pioneers—black and white—made the difficult trek to the French Lick, the future site of Nashville.

1780	The battle at Kings Mountain was a key American victory during the Revolutionary War. The Tennessee militia played an important part in this victory.
1784	The State of Franklin was formed in east Tennessee. This short-lived State of Franklin passed out of existence in 1788.
1789	North Carolina ceded its western land, the Tennessee county, to the Federal Government. Congress now designated the area as territory of the United States, south of the Ohio River.
1796	On June 1, 1796, Congress approved the admission of Tennessee as the sixteenth state of the Union.
1815	On January 8th, Andrew Jackson and his Tennessean troops defeated the British army at the Battle of New Orleans.
1818	The Chickasaw Treaty of 1818 extended Tennessee's western boundary to the Mississippi River, and opened up a rich, new agricultural area for settlement.
1826	The state capitol moved to its permanent site in Nashville.
1828	Andrew Jackson was elected president of the United States by landslide majorities in 1828 and 1832.
1838	The U.S. Army was dispatched to evict the Cherokee and send them on a woeful trek to Indian Territory—the "Trail of Tears".
1844	James K. Polk of Maury County was elected president.
1861	Having ratified its connection to the fledgling Confederacy by popular vote, Tennessee became the last state to withdraw from the Union.
1861–1865	187,000 Confederate and 51,000 Federal soldiers mustered in from Tennessee as the Civil War raged throughout the South.
1865	Andrew Johnson became president following Lincoln's assassination in April.

1866	Tennessee was readmitted to the Union after it became the third state to ratify the Fourteenth Amendment.
1870	Delegates from across the state met in 1870 to rewrite the Constitution.
1880	Englishman Thomas Hughes established the Rugby colony.
1894	Ruskin, another experimental colony, was founded in 1894 by the famous socialist publicist Julius Wayland.
1897	The Tennessee Centennial Exposition was held in Nashville in honor of the state's 100th birthday.
1898	Four regiments of Tennesseans were called in to the volunteer United States Army during the Spanish-American War.
1917–1918	Around 100,000 of the state's young men volunteered or were drafted into the armed services during World War I.
1920	Tennessee became the 36th state to ratify the Nineteenth Amendment, giving women the right to vote.
1925	The celebrated trial of John T. Scopes, the so-called "Monkey Trial," took place in Dayton.
1925	Reelfoot Lake was established as a state game and fish preserve, marking the first step toward the conservation of Tennessee's natural resources.
1933	The Tennessee Valley Authority built its first hydroelectric dams in Tennessee.
1940	The Great Smoky Mountains National Park was dedicated by President Franklin Roosevelt.
1941–1945	During World War II, over 300,000 Tennesseans served in the armed forces while others served at home in war-related industries.
1950–1953	10,500 Tennesseans served in the Korean War.

1953	The Tennessee State Library and Archives building was dedicated to the men and women from Tennessee who served in WWII.
1960	Students held the first Nashville sit-in at downtown luncheon counters.
1965	A. W. Willis, Jr., from Memphis, became the first African American representative elected to the General Assembly in 65 years.
1968	Dr. Martin Luther King, Jr. was assassinated at the Lorraine Motel in Memphis, where he went in support of the strike of the local sanitation workers.
1977	Tennessean Alex Hailey won the Nobel Prize for his book *Roots*.
1987	General Motors opened the new Saturn Corporation auto plant in Spring Hill.
1990	Martha Craig Daughtrey became the first woman to serve on the Tennessee Supreme Court.
1992	Albert Gore, Jr. was elected Vice-President of the United States.
1998	The University of Tennessee football team became national champions, going undefeated for the season.
2002	Former Nashville Mayor Phil Bredesen was elected Governor.
2007	Steven Cohen was elected into Congress.

The Geography Of Tennessee

Tennessee is located in the southeast central region of the United States, lying between the Mississippi River on the west and the Blue Ridge and Appalachian Mountains on the east.

Tennessee is divided into three **Grand Divisions**, which are recognized under state law as East Tennessee, Middle Tennessee, and West Tennessee. The Grand Divisions vary in land and culture.

East Tennessee has a rugged terrain covered with dense forest and brush. This Grand Division includes the Great Smoky Mountains, which are a part of the Cumberland Plateau region, and the Unaka Mountains. East Tennessee remained largely isolated from the outside world until the early 20th century. This area is also covered by fertile valleys and wooded ridges.

The next Grand division is Middle Tennessee. Middle Tennessee stretches from the Cumberland Plateau on the east to the Tennessee River on the west. This Grand division is full of beautiful, fertile bluegrass land, which makes it ideal for dairy farming, raising livestock and breeding superior horses.

The last of the three Grand Divisions is West Tennessee. Most of this land is flat and easy to farm. The Tennessee River is the beginning of western Tennessee, and it continues to the Mississippi River. West Tennessee thrives on the Mississippi River, which nurtures the area's largest farmland. In western Tennessee, cotton has historically been the leading crop.

Tennessee can also be divided into **six geological regions**. Each of the six regions is characterized by a specific landform. Starting from the east, the **Unaka or Blue Ridge Mountains** are home to the highest mountains

Great Smokey Mountains National Park, TN

in Tennessee, the Smoky Mountains. The **Appalachian Ridge and Valley** runs from Chattanooga to Knoxville.

The Appalachian Mountains include several mountains including Lookout Mountain, where there is an amazing view of seven states. The land was not good farming land, so the people living in isolation in the hills had plenty of time to devote to their craft, music and artwork.

Next is the **Cumberland Plateau**, where the beautiful Cumberland Gap is nestled. The Cumberland Plateau is covered with steep flat-topped mountains, cliffs and narrow valleys. It is 450 miles long and 50 miles wide and lies between the Appalachian Ridge and Valley region to the east and the rolling plains to the west. The region is divided by the Cumberland and Kentucky rivers and by tributaries of the Tennessee River. There are large deposits of coal, limestone, and sandstone in the plateau.

The Cumberland Gap is a 1,640-foot long natural pass that goes through the Cumberland Plateau. There are many cliffs in this region, which make it difficult to penetrate. The Gap includes the Wilderness Road, blazed by Daniel Boone, which became the main passageway that opened the Northwest Territory for settlers.

Middle Tennessee is known for the **Central basin**. The Central basin is a large, bowl-shaped depression that was once under an ocean; this makes the soil lush and fertile. The Central basin has a 300-foot descent. It is home to the Cumberland River and Cumberland Bluffs. Because the capital city is located in the Central Basin, it is sometimes referred to as Nashville Basin.

The **Highland Rim** is the high ground that circles the Central Basin. Last, there is the **Gulf Coast Plain**. It extends from the Tennessee River to the Mississippi River. This area thrives on the Mississippi River making it a splendid agricultural region.

One cannot discuss Tennessee without mentioning the Mississippi River. In fact,

Mississippi River - bridge at night

all the major rivers of Tennessee lie within the huge Mississippi River system, such as the Little Tennessee, Clinch, Big Sandy, and Duck Rivers. However, the most important rivers are the Mississippi River, along the state's western border, and the Tennessee and Cumberland Rivers to the east.

Tennessee has **five major cities**. Over the years, Tennessee's population and industrial growth have made these cities **metropolises**. Starting in the east, **Knoxville** and **Chattanooga** have rich historical presence. **Knoxville** is the site of the oldest and largest campus, the University of Tennessee.

Knoxville

In 1863, Confederate and Union soldiers battled on Lookout Mountain in **Chattanooga**. Then there is **Nashville,** the state capital. Located in Middle Tennessee, Nashville is known as the national capital of country music. This region is also home to many colleges. **Jackson's** namesake, President Andrew Jackson, purchased the city from the Chickasaw in 1818.

Memphis is the hub of West Tennessee, home to the Fed Ex Headquarters. Its history is conjoined to the Mississippi River and is also believed to be the origin of blues music.

Tennessee has an abundance of **natural resources**, such as lumber. Most of

Tennessee's forests are found in East Tennessee. **Coal** is also found in the eastern part of the state in the Cumberland Plateau. **Zinc** is mined near Knoxville and Clarksville in middle Tennessee. **Copper** is found near the Appalachian Mountains in the east. **Natural gas** is found near Nashville in the Highland Rim and the Cumberland Plateau.

Lastly, one of the most important resources is water. The many dams across the state provide **hydroelectric power**, which supplies electricity to seven states and three million people.

The plants and animals in Tennessee make the state even more enjoyable to live in. Today, forests cover about half of the state. Many tree species are found throughout Tennessee's forests such as the hickory, tulip poplar, or tulip tree, which is the state tree, and the red maple, sycamore, elm, and pine tree.

The bison, wolves, and elk that once roamed in these forests have now disappeared from the state. However, you can still find black bear, white-tailed deer, and cougar.

There are smaller mammals, such as red fox, beaver, mink, raccoon, skunk, weasel, and opossum. Other small mammals also found in Tennessee include muskrat, woodchuck, cottontail, swamp rabbit, gray fox, and southern flying squirrel. Recently, red wolves were reintroduced into the Great Smoky Mountains National Park.

Tennessee is no doubt one of the country's most beautiful and diverse states. If you wanted to vacation in Tennessee, you would be amazed by the variety of choices in the scenery. With its awesome mountains and sparkling rivers, you couldn't find a more appealing landscape than Tennessee.

Terms to Know

basin: a large, bowl-shaped depression in the surface of the land or ocean floor.

compass rose: a design used on maps to indicate the points of the compass.

geology: the study of the earth.

lake: a large inland body of fresh water or salt water.

map key: (also known as a map legend) a table of symbols used on a map or chart.

metropolis: a major city, especially the chief city of a country or region.

mountain range: a series of mountain ridges alike in form, direction, and origin.

plateau: an elevated, comparatively level expanse of land; a tableland.

river: a large natural stream of water emptying into an ocean, lake, or other body of water and usually fed along its course by converging tributaries.

scale: a system of ordered marks at fixed intervals used as a reference standard in measurement.

Activities

1. On a blank map, locate where you live in Tennessee and find the distance from your home to the Cumberland Plateau or the Mississippi River.
2. Make a mobile of the animals found in Tennessee.
3. Use color pencils and a blank map to identify the three Grand Divisions of Tennessee.
4. Write a paragraph describing the location of your community and how the region affects your way of life.
5. Use a T-chart to list Tennessee's natural resources and their uses.
6. Locate the six geological regions of Tennessee on a map.

Want to Know More?

Web Sites

www.enchantedlearning.com/usa/states/tennessee

www.50states.com/tennesse.htm

www.destination360.com/north-america/us/tennessee/history.php

www.state.tn.us/education/webfacts.shtml

Correlations

Performance Indicators State

6.3.spi.1.	7.3.spi.5.
6.3.spi.2.	7.3.spi.7.
6.3.spi.5.	7.3.spi.12.
7.3.spi.3.	8.3.spi.2.

Correlations to McDougal Littell Textbooks

World History: Ancient Civilizations, pp. 9-12, 14-23, 78-79, 82-87, 96, 108-109, 118-127, 142-143, 146-153, 188-193, 202-207, 218-224, 248-249, 252-257, 284-285, 288-293, 342-347, 350-351, 354-359, 398-403, 426-427, 430-435

World History: Medieval and Early Modern Times, pp. 14-21

World Cultures and Geography, pp. A19, A21, 43-45, 61, 109, 126, 128-129, 149

American History: Beginnings Through Reconstruction, pp. A12–A13, 113, 350–351

The First Inhabitants of Tennessee: Three Mighty Tribes

About 12,000 years ago, several different Native American cultures flourished in Tennessee, including Paleo-Indians. Divided into small bands, they roamed widely over the land, hunting many now-extinct animals such as mammoths and saber-toothed big cats.

About 8,000 to 2,500 years ago, Tennessee's inhabitants began weaving baskets and making highly specialized stone tools. Beginning about 2,500 years ago, people of the Woodland **culture** practiced horticulture. They also made clay pottery and built mounds, used for important **rituals**. Mounds remaining from this period still exist in many parts of Tennessee such as Memphis's Chucalissa Village.

It is thought that around 800 A.D., a great **agricultural** society of mound builders, called the Mississippian or Temple Mound culture, arose in the Southeast. Mississippian peoples constructed great dirt burial mounds. They also built massive earthworks that supported temples and rulers' residences.

Across the Mississippi River from present-day St. Louis, Missouri, the Mississippians built one of the largest villages, Cahokia, which may have been home to 20,000 or more people.

There were many tribes that thrived in the Tennessee area. However, **Creek, Cherokee and Chickasaw** were some of the most famous. Before Europeans arrived in North America, the Creek, Cherokee and Chickasaw controlled a large region of the Southeast: the Cherokee in the east, Creeks in middle Tennessee and the Chickasaw in the west. Although each tribe had its own language, culture and traditions, these three great societies lived in harmony.

The Cherokee Indians lived in small communities, usually located in fertile river bottoms. The word *Tennessee* is believed to derive from *Tanasi,* the name of a Cherokee village on the Little Tennessee River. Cherokee homes were wooden frames covered with woven vines and saplings plastered with mud.

Each village consisted of up to 50 log and mud huts grouped around the town square, called the Council House, where ceremonial and public meetings were held. The council house was seven-sided to represent the seven clans of the Cherokee: Bird, Paint, Deer, Wolf, Blue, Long Hair, and Wild Potato.

Each tribe elected two chiefs— a peace chief who counseled during peaceful times, and a war chief who made decisions during times of war. However, the chiefs did not have absolute rule. Decision-making was a more democratic process, with tribal members having the opportunity to voice concerns.

Nikwasi Indian Mound

Because of their intelligence, the Cherokee not only developed a practical political system; they created their own alphabet. **Sequoia,** a wise Tennessee-born Cherokee, created a written document with the tribe's syllables.

The Cherokee Indian society was a matriarchy. The children took the clan of the mother, and kinship was traced through the mother's family. Women had an equal voice in the affairs of the tribe. Marriage was only allowed between members of different clans, and property was passed on according to clan alliance.

The Chickasaw mainly lived on the Mississippi River at Chickasaw Bluffs, now the site of Memphis, Tennessee. The Chickasaw were a patriarchal society that was known for its war-like disposition as they were constantly fighting with the neighboring tribes.

All three of the tribes were expert hunters, fishermen and farmers. They were also the first conservationists. They believed in using every part of the animals they killed and only killed for necessity. Deer hides were used for pants and shoes, called moccasins. Leather and fur were saved for the winter months. The tribes found nuts, berries and fruit and also planted **maize**.

By the time European explorers and traders arrived, the Cherokee, Creek, and Chickasaw lands covered a large part of the southeastern United States, including Tennessee. Spanish explorer Hernando de Soto led an exploration through Cherokee territory in 1540. When explorers opened the door of east and west Tennessee in the sixteenth century, they encountered these three wonderful Mississippian cultures. Sadly, by the beginning of the seventeenth century, Mississippian cultures were scarce due to European diseases and warfare.

In the late eighteenth century, as the European settlers arrived in large numbers, conflicts increased. The Cherokee, Creek, and Chickasaw fought with settlers, but eventually withdrew to the mountains or were pushed further west.

If the tribes thought things could not get any worse, they were sadly mistaken. They were forced to sign over much of their land, first to the British, and then to the United States. Eventually, war and disease decimated the tribes.

Terms to Know

archaeologist: a person who studies past human life and culture by the recovery and examination of remaining material evidence, such as graves, buildings, tools, and pottery.

culture: the predominating attitudes and behavior that characterize the functioning of a group or organization.

maize: Indian corn.

Native American: a member of any of the indigenous peoples of the Western Hemisphere.

nomad: a member of a group of people who have no fixed home and move according to the seasons from place to place in search of food, water, and grazing land.

religion: a set of beliefs, values, and practices based on the teachings of a spiritual leader.

ritual: a ceremonial act or a series of such acts.

tradition: the passing down of elements of a culture from generation to generation, especially by oral communication.

Activities

1. Make your own postage stamp to remember a favorite fact about one of the tribes of Tennessee.

2. On a blank map, locate where you live in Tennessee and where the Mississippi River is located.

3. Using a T-chart, compare Native American mounds to our present day ritual sites.

Want to Know More?

Web Sites

www.state.tn.us/sos/symbols/facts.htm

www.infoplease.com/ipa/A0108274.html

www.libraryspot.com/state/tn.htm

www.50states.com/tennesse.htm

www.destination360.com/north-america/us/tennessee/history.php

www.state.tn.us/education/webfacts.shtml

Correlations

Performance Indicators State

6.1.spi.2.	7.1.spi.1.
6.1.spi.5.	8.1.spi.1.
6.1.spi.6.	

Correlations to McDougal Littell Textbooks

World History: Ancient Civilizations, pp. 9-12, 15-23, 27-33, 34-37, 39-43, 54-55, 82-86, 89-95, 99-103, 146-151, 155-161, 188-193, 218-224, 252-257, 277-280, 288-293, 354-359, 361-365, 411-417, 430-435

World History: Medieval and Early Modern Times, pp. 9-13, 25-28, 31-35, 46-51, 58-65, 84-89, 98-105, 130-139, 156-169, 180-184, 186-199, 194-201, 212-221, 226, 232-237, 266-273, 298-305, 366-371, 394-407, 408-417, 434-443, 470-477, 520-527

World Cultures and Geography, pp. 80, 89-90, 92-93, 94-95, 110, 111, 148, 191, 192-195, 234, 237, 260, 264, 293, 294, 318, 319-323, 410, 416, 435, 443, 455, 456-457, 488, 507, 522, 527, 528-533, 573, 584, 614, 627, 635, 646, 647-649, 678, 679, 680, 685, 714-715, 718, 739, 751, 752-753, 777, 779, 780, 786, 809, 816, 832, 838-839, 842, 843, 878-879, 880-881, 895, 897, R38-R54

American History: Beginnings Through Reconstruction, pp. 70, 72, 79

Hernando de Soto and Other Tennessee Explorers

Historians believe an expedition led by Hernando de Soto in 1540 conducted the earliest exploration of Tennessee by non-Native Americans. The expedition of some seven hundred Spaniards and their slaves landed at Tampa Bay and moved north in search of food and gold.

The expedition turned west in mid-May, crossing the Blue Ridge Mountains. Following a trail through the mountains, they came upon the town of Chiaha on Zimmerman's Island in the French Broad River near modern Dandridge. After a short rest, de Soto headed to the small village of Chiscas.

The hospitable Chiahans provided the Spaniards with food and played and swam with them in the French Broad River. However, the hospitality ran out when de Soto asked for thirty women to take with him. De Soto's demand for women brought an end to the peaceful relations.

Rather than fight the Spaniards, the Chiahans left their town early one morning and took refuge on a nearby island in hopes the Spaniards would leave. De Soto tried to hunt the Chiahans down, but was unable to reach the **refuge** by horse. De Soto and the Chiahans negotiated a **truce** that gave the Spaniards porters, but no women.

De Soto finally left Chiaha, passing through several neighboring towns along the Tennessee River. In the town of Coste, the chief personally escorted de Soto through his towns to show his hospitality. At the Coste capital, near the mouth of the Little Tennessee River, de Soto took the chief hostage in order to obtain guides and porters and to prevent bloodshed after his men pillaged the farms and houses.

Hernando de Soto

Later that summer, de Soto left Coste. Near present day Sweetwater, the expedition again replenished their supplies with corn, beans, and other food. Crossing the Hiwassee River, they reached the town of Tasqui, near modern Conasauga, Tennessee. De Soto continued to push on.

De Soto apparently turned back to the southwest before heading north again and entering the bounds of Tennessee south of Memphis. He crossed the Mississippi River and continued exploring to the west. As the health and spirits of his men deteriorated, de Soto brought them back to the Mississippi River, where he died from a fever.

Other Explorers in Tennessee

There were other explores who came to Tennessee in search of riches and fame. Juan Pardo, a Spanish explorer, was no exception. Pardo explored areas of Tennessee from 1566

Louis Joliet and Jacques Marquette

to 1567 in search of gold. He also wanted to establish alliances with native tribes. He never found gold, nor did he become friendly with the Native Americans. However, his expedition maintained a detailed written description of the land and its inhabitants of Tennessee.

Later, in 1673, a French expedition under the command of Father Jacques Marquette, a Jesuit missionary, and Louis Joliet, a fur trader, sailed the Mississippi River, stopping along the way at Chickasaw Bluffs near present-day Memphis.

In 1682 another French expedition, led by Robert de La Salle, explored the Mississippi River and built a fort near the mouth of the Hatchie River. La Salle's **explorations** made way for the French to extend their trading network further into the continent.

As a result, by 1692, French traders had established posts along the Cumberland River near a salt springs. This **post** became known as the French Lick and in 1780, served as the center for the Nashville settlements.

Exploring the wilderness was dangerous and uncertain. Englishmen James Needham and Gabriel Arthur are tragic examples. While traveling in what is now upper east Tennessee to establish trading relations with the Cherokee, Needham, unfamiliar with the **customs** of the Cherokee, angered the tribe and was killed.

However, his comrade Arthur remained with the tribe for over a year, building a trading relationship that would continue through the next century.

Another explorer who left his imprint on Tennessee was Dr. Thomas Walker. The Loyal Land Company, which located and claimed lands, sent Walker to the Tennessee region. Walker was a leading shareholder in the company. In 1750, Walker's expedition passed through the **Cumberland Gap**, crossed the **Cumberland Plateau**, and sailed down the **Cumberland River**, all of which he named in honor of the Duke of Cumberland. Walker became one of the wealthiest men of his time.

Long hunters, or frontiersmen, were also explorers. Unlike the explorers that came before them, long hunters sought furs. Their expeditions led them across the Blue Ridge and Appalachian Mountains, hunting and trapping.

The best-known long hunters were Daniel Boone, Kasper Mansker, Bledsoe, Stone, and Thomas Sharp "Bigfoot" Spencer. Areas were named after these legendary men. These pioneers brought back tales of rich land and plentiful game, which helped encourage settlement in Tennessee.

Terms to Know

alliance: a formal agreement establishing such an association, especially an international treaty of friendship.

custom: a practice followed by people of a particular group or region.

Cumberland Gap: a natural passage through the Cumberland Plateau near the junction of the Kentucky, Virginia, and Tennessee borders. It was used by Daniel Boone in 1775 as a strategic point along his Wilderness Road, the principal route of westward migration for the next half century.

Cumberland Plateau: the southwest section of the Appalachian Mountains, extending northeast to southwest from southern West Virginia through Virginia, Kentucky, and Tennessee into northern Alabama.

exploration: to search into or travel in for the purpose of discovery.

long hunter: a man who lives on the frontier.

post: a trading post.

refuge: a place providing protection or shelter.

truce: a temporary suspension of hostilities by agreement of the opposing sides.

Activities

1. Create a timeline of Tennessee's early exploration.

2. Locate where you live in Tennessee on a blank map.

3. Use color pencils and a blank map to identify the Cumberland River, Cumberland Gap and Cumberland Plateau.

4. Write a paragraph describing the location of your community and how the region affects your way of life.

Want to Know More?

Websites

www.state.tn.us/sos/symbols/facts.htm

www.infoplease.com/ipa/A0108274.html

www.libraryspot.com/state/tn.htm

www.50states.com/tennesse.htm

www.destination360.com/north-america/us/tennessee/history.php

www.state.tn.us/education/webfacts.shtml

www.encarta.msn.com/encyclopedia

www.en.wikipedia.org/wiki/Dictionary

Correlations

Performance Indicators State

6.3.spi.1.	7.3.spi.10.
6.3.spi.2.	7.3.spi.12.
6.3.spi.5.	8.3.spi.1.
7.3.spi.3.	8.3.spi.2.
7.3.spi.4.	8.3.spi.3.
7.3.spi.5.	8.3.spi.5.
7.3.spi.7.	8.3.spi.6.
7.3.spi.9.	8.3.spi.7.

Correlations to McDougal Littell Textbooks

World History: Ancient Civilizations, pp. 9-12, 14-23, 78-79, 82-87, 96, 108-109, 118-127, 142-143, 146-153, 188-193, 202-207, 218-224, 248-249, 252-257, 284-285, 288-293, 342-347, 350-351, 354-359, 398-403, 426-427, 430-435

World History: Medieval and Early Modern Times, pp. 14-21

World Cultures and Geography, pp. A5, A11, A14-A15, A18-A19, A21-A22, A24, A26-A27, A30, A32-A33, A36-A37, 6, 34-39, 42-45, 58, 61, 63, 69, 94-95, 109, 122, 124-129, 149, 156-159, 198-201, 204-208, 326-329, 459-463, 496-499, 535-539, 627, 652-655, 658-662, 755-759, 795-799, 824-828, 851-854, 883-887, 912-914, 920-923

American History: Beginnings Through Reconstruction, pp. A12–A13, 4–11, 63–64, 66–75, 79–88, 95–96, 98–99, 103–109, 111–115, 117–119, 134–135, 246, 350–351, 372, 375, 381-382, 453

Moving West: How Tennessee Was Established

The story of America is a story of movement. Movement west caused many conflicts among the Native American, French, British and Tennessee settlers. Both Britain and France claimed the Tennessee territory, causing conflict that erupted into war.

Many **alliances** were formed between the Native Americans and European countries. In 1763, the war ended and France lost control of its lands in North America. Naturally, because many of the colonists had fought in the war, they decided to settle the land.

Historians believe the first European settler in Tennessee was William Bean. Bean built a log cabin in East Tennessee along the Watauga River. Just one year later, one thousand settlers had joined him. Pioneers continued to move into the Tennessee area in droves. Among the most famous was Daniel Boone.

Daniel Boone was likely the best-known frontiersman or long hunter in Tennessee at the time. Boone blazed a trail across the Appalachian Mountains to hunt and explore the area of present-day Tennessee.

Boone had heard of rich lands and abundant game west of the mountains. During the mid 1700s, he began exploring across the Blue Ridge Mountains into what is now upper east Tennessee. It is thought that Boone recorded his presence in Washington County in 1760, when he carved the inscription, *Cilled a Bar* on a tree.

In 1775, Boone helped to build the first road through the mountains to the Cumberland Gap, which became the main route that opened the Northwest Territory.

The settlers' encroachment on the Native Americans

Daniel Boone

Cumberland

made life uneasy for the natives and the settlers. As a result, The British issued a **proclamation** establishing a border down the crest of the **Appalachian Mountains**. The proclamation stated that land west of the line was designated for Cherokees and other Native Americans. However, settlers still continued to move west and fight with the natives.

The government then made **treaties** with the Native Americans promising fair treatment. Soon, these treaties were broken as well. This made the Native Americans mistrust settlers even more.

During this time, settlements along the Watauga and Nolichucky rivers created the **Watauga Association** in order to maintain peace and protect themselves from Cherokee attacks. Pioneers at the French Lick on the Cumberland River drew up the Cumberland Compact for similar purposes.

The **Cumberland Compact** was an agreement in which two men were chosen to represent the fort. There was also a committee that made laws for the settlers to follow. Despite these efforts, life was still dangerous. The Creek and Cherokee Indians often attacked the settlers.

Still, the settlers remained determined to make a life in the wilderness. Eventually, these small settlements wanted to form a new state.

Supporters of statehood petitioned Congress to influence North Carolina to release control of its western lands. North Carolina would not budge, but settlers continued to forge on. They hoped Congress would approve of a new, separate state named for Pennsylvania's Benjamin Franklin with or without North Carolina's cooperation.

John Sevier assumed leadership of the State of Franklin. A pioneer, soldier, statesman and a founder of the Republic, he was Tennessee's first governor. John Sevier also was the first and only governor of Franklin. Sevier served six terms as governor of Tennessee.

Sevier was a true pioneer who fought through the wilderness to shape the State of Tennessee. Today a statue in Nashville honors Governor Sevier. He served as governor of Franklin under a constitution that closely resembled that of North Carolina.

Sadly, the **State of Franklin** failed, dying slowly over a period of several years, a victim of North Carolina's opposition and Congress's lack of support.

Finally, on December 12, 1789, North Carolina lawmakers passed another act transferring western land to the new national government under the U.S. Constitution. This was the Northwest Ordinance of 1787. The ordinance held forth the promise of statehood for the future Tennessee. So on June 1, 1796, Tennessee became the sixteenth state in the **Union**.

Terms to Know

alliance: a formal agreement establishing such an association, especially an international treaty of friendship.

Appalachian Mountains: a mountain system of eastern North America extending about 2,574 km (1,600 mi) southwest from Newfoundland, New Brunswick, and southern Quebec, Canada, to central Alabama. The range includes the Allegheny, Blue Ridge, and Cumberland mountains.

Cumberland Compact: the Cumberland Compact is articles of agreement created in 1780 by settlers when they arrived on the Cumberland River and settled Fort Nashborough, which would become Nashville, Tennessee.

Cumberland Gap: a natural passage through the Cumberland Plateau near the junction of the Kentucky, Virginia, and Tennessee borders. It was used by Daniel Boone in 1775 as a strategic point along his Wilderness Road, the principal route of westward migration for the next half century.

Daniel Boone: American frontiersman, folk hero, and central figure in the settlement of Kentucky.

frontier: an undeveloped area or field for discovery or research.

John Sevier: served four years (1785–1789) as the only governor of the State of Franklin and twelve years (1796–1801 and 1803–1809) as Governor of Tennessee, and as a U.S. Representative from Tennessee from 1811 until his death.

long hunter: an eighteenth century explorer and hunter who made expeditions into the American frontier wilderness for as much as six months at a time.

proclamation: something proclaimed, especially an official public announcement.

State of Franklin: an autonomous, secessionist United States territory created from territory that later was ceded by North Carolina to the federal government. The territory comprising Franklin later became part of the state of Tennessee. Franklin was never officially admitted into the Union of the United States and existed for only four years.

Union: the United States of America regarded as a national unit.

Activities

1. Create a diary for a child on the frontier.

2. Write an essay about Native American life.

3. Have groups of students write a classroom compact. The compare compacts on a Venn diagram.

4. On a blank map, locate the Appalachian Mountains and Cumberland Gap and discuss the significance of the Cumberland Gap in Tennessee history.

Want to Know More?

Web Sites

www.enchantedlearning.com

www.en.wikipedia.org/wiki/Dictionary

www.state.tn.us/sos/symbols/facts.htm

www.libraryspot.com/state/tn.htm

www.50states.com/tennesse.htm

www.destination360.com/north-america/us/tennessee/history.php

www.state.tn.us/education/webfacts.shtml

Correlations

Performance Indicators State

6.4.spi.2.	8.3.spi.6.
6.4.spi.3.	8.4.spi.9.
6.4.spi.4.	8.5.spi.13.
7.4.spi.3.	

Expansion in Tennessee

Thousands of pioneers moved to Tennessee to obtain cheap land. Unfortunately, the land was mostly wilderness. Settlers cleared the land and established rural settlements all over Tennessee.

East Tennessee was largely an area of small subsistence farming. Middle Tennessee, with its beautiful bluegrass pastures, produced thoroughbred horses and livestock. Tobacco, cotton and corn were also grown in the area. West Tennessee's fertile lowlands and huge plantations produced vast amounts of cotton. Memphis, founded in 1819, quickly became one of the largest and most lucrative commercial cotton producing cities.

Unfortunately, the new state of Tennessee inherited some old problems, such as **slavery**. When North Carolina ceded its western lands to the United States in 1790, certain stipulations were negotiated, such as slavery. Therefore, when Tennessee achieved statehood, it operated under the laws first published by North Carolina, in which slaves were regarded as property.

Life was hard for slaves; and in Tennessee it was no different. Slaves worked from sun up to sun down planting, harvesting crops, and tending to farm animals.

However, not all Africans were slaves. In some isolated cases, Africans were free and owned their own businesses and homes. Often it was short-lived because of hostility and prejudice. Fortunately, slavery officially ended in Tennessee in April of 1865.

Africans were not the only group treated unfairly in Tennessee; Native Americans were forced to leave the land on which they had lived for thousand of years. Moreover, the enforcer of the act was our seventh president and Tennessee native, **Andrew Jackson**.

At the time, whites believed the Cherokees were the biggest obstacle blocking them from their destiny of possessing Tennessee, Georgia, North Carolina, and Alabama.

In 1828, Andrew Jackson, whose pioneer experiences had resulted in deep resentment against all Native Americans, was elected president of the United States. In his inaugural address, Jackson called for the **relocation** of all eastern Indians beyond the Mississippi River.

Andrew Jackson

A popular idea among white settlers, this presidential wish became federal law with the passing of the **Indian Removal Act in 1830.**

Not all settlers agreed with Andrew Jackson. **Davy Crockett** and **Sam Houston** are two examples. Crockett openly and strongly opposed President Andrew Jackson's policies concerning the Indian Removal Bill of 1830.

Sam Houston was also opposed to the removal of the Cherokee Nation. As a child, Houston lived with a band of Cherokees for long periods of time. Their leader, Chief

Sam Houston

Davy Crockett

Oolooteka, became a surrogate father, teaching Houston the language and ways of the Cherokees. However, unlike Davy Crockett, Houston never spoke up for the Cherokee because Andrew Jackson was his close friend. Later, Sam Houston became governor of Tennessee and president of independent Texas.

Davy Crockett was a Tennessee frontiersman. He was also a Tennessee legislator, U.S. congressman, and folk hero. Crockett lived in Tennessee for all but the last few months of his life and promoted the gradual westward expansion of the frontier through Tennessee toward Texas.

Crockett served as a justice of the peace, a colonel of the fifty-seventh militia regiment, and in 1821 was elected to the Tennessee legislature. He was elected to the U.S. House of Representatives from his new west Tennessee residence in 1827. He campaigned

as a straightforward country boy and an extraordinary hunter and marksman.

At the time, pioneers longed to hear tales about courageous frontiersmen. Crockett knew this and added tall tales to his adventures. Crockett's popularity grew and grew, until he became a living legend.

Being a true frontiersman, his fame could not bring an end to his inevitable spirit to explore new lands and conquer the wilderness. This spirit led him to Texas. Unfortunately, Crockett met his fate at the Alamo in San Antonio, Texas. He died in battle on March 6, 1836 as a legendary Tennessee hero.

Soon after that tragic event, another sad episode in Tennessee's history took place: **The Trail of Tears,** or *Nunna daul Isunyi* in the Cherokee language, which means "The Trail Where We Cried". The Trail of Tears was a tragic journey the proud Cherokee Nation took when they were forced to leave their beloved homeland in Tennessee for Oklahoma. They marched from May 1838 to March 1839.

James Polk

Not all was bad in the new state of Tennessee. **Expansion** of the United States looked unstoppable. Americans believed they would one day own the entire North American continent. President James K. Polk, former Tennessee governor, wanted to help that aspiration come true.

Excitedly, because of statehood, thousands of settlers rushed in to claim cheap, bountiful land. As a result, towns and cities cropped up all over Tennessee's wilderness.

Soon the industry changed in Tennessee. Railroads and steamboats assisted in **industrial** growth, such as the export of timber, iron, coal and copper from east Tennessee. In Knoxville and Nashville, textiles were produced. Flour, meal, dairy and cotton goods were grown in west Tennessee. Jack Daniels liquor and tobacco products were produced in middle Tennessee.

The boost in the **economy** made life better for Tennesseans. By the end of the 1860s, Tennessee's population had grown to one million people.

Terms to Know

Davy Crockett: American folk hero, frontiersman, soldier and politician; usually referred by the popular title "King of the Wild Frontier". He represented Tennessee in the U.S. House of Representatives, served in the Texas Revolution, and died at the age of 49 at the Battle of the Alamo.

economy: careful, thrifty management of resources, such as money, materials, or labor.

expansion: the act or process of expanding: *the new nation's expansion westward.*

industry: commercial production and sale of goods.

Native American: a member of any of the indigenous peoples of the Western Hemisphere.

population: all of the people inhabiting a specified area.

prejudice: irrational suspicion or hatred of a particular group, race, or religion.

relocation: to move to or establish in a new place.

Sam Houston: an American statesman, politician, and soldier born in Rockbridge County, Virginia. His earlier life included encouraging emigration to Tennessee, time spent with the Cherokee Nation (into which he was adopted and later married into), and subsequent successful involvement in Tennessee politics.

slavery: holding persons against their will to perform free labor.

Activities

1. Write an essay describing how it would feel if you were forced to leave your home.

2. Using a T-chart, list natural resources and goods and how they affect your life.

3. Create a Venn diagram, noting the similarities and differences between the two tragic events mentioned above.

4. Draw a picture of Davy Crockett including the items a frontiersman would need to survive.

Want to Know More?

Web Sites

tnhistoryforkids.org/

tennesseeencyclopedia.net/

www.tennesseehistory.org/

Correlations

Performance Indicators State

6.3.spi.6.	7.4.spi.3.
6.4.spi.1.	7.3.spi.9.
6.6.spi.1.	8.4.spi.2.
7.2.spi.3.	8.4.spi.9.
7.3.spi.5.	8.5.spi.13.

Correlations to McDougal Littell Textbooks

World History: Ancient Civilizations, pp. 112-117, 118-127, 128-135, 154-163, 172-181, 188-195, 226-231, 232-239, 258-265, 266-275, 304, 325-329, 370-377, 378-385, 436-441, 487, 502-505, 514-521, R13

World History: Medieval and Early Modern Times, pp. S16, 46-51, 55-56, 58-65, 112-117, 118-129, 130-139, 164-173, 194-201, 222-231, 232-237, 238-243, 266-273, 298-305, 306-313, 321-325, 534-541, 542-553, R13

World Cultures and Geography, pp. A14-A15, A18-A19, A22, A24, A26-A27, A30, A32-A33, A36, A37, 34, 35-39, 59-63, 64-65, 85, 109, 122, 124, 125, 126-127, 128-129, 149, 156, 157-159, 198, 199-201, 204, 205-208, 326, 327-329, 459, 460, 461-463, 496, 497-499, 535, 536, 537-539, 652, 653-654, 655, 658, 659-662, 755, 756, 757-759, 795, 796, 797-799, 824, 825-828, 851, 852, 853-854, 883, 884, 885-887, 912, 913-914, 920, 921-923

American History: Beginnings Through Reconstruction, pp. 68, 69, 71, 73, 74, 75, 138, 139, 140, 234–241, 245–246, 250–252, 255, 256, 262–265, 262–265, 266–285, 266–299, 384, 395, 396–398, 400–401, 402–407, 408–412, 429–431, 432–437, 486, 488, 502

The Industrial Revolution and the Civil War in Tennessee

During the early 1800s, life began to change all over the United States. This change was called the **Industrial Revolution**.

Technology made life faster and easier, making slave labor less of a necessity. Many Northerners began working in factories instead of farms. Life in the South, however, did not change as drastically. Most people still lived and worked on farms. As time passed, the North and the South began to have different economies and social ways of life.

These differences also applied to the three Grand Divisions of Tennessee. East Tennessee was filled with hills and mountains, and therefore did not require many slaves. As a result, East Tennesseans supported ending slavery.

Middle Tennessee, where grain, cattle, and tobacco grew, required thousands of slaves. West Tennessee, the area between the Tennessee and Mississippi Rivers, produced thousands of bails of cotton, also requiring slaves. Therefore, people living in Middle and West Tennessee believed slavery should continue.

The nation's conflict and impending war put a halt to Tennessee's industrial revolution. War was on everyone's mind—not progress.

In 1857 the slave **Dred Scott** sued for his freedom in the Supreme Court. Scott lost; the Court claimed that Scott was not a citizen and could not sue in a U.S. court. Abraham

Lincoln, a presidential candidate, debated and argued that the court decision was morally, socially, and politically wrong.

In 1860 **Abraham Lincoln** was elected president. Because of his views on slavery, many Southern states wanted to leave the **Union** and form their own country called the **Confederacy**. In 1861, some of those states did **secede**, but Tennessee was unsure which side to take. In East Tennessee, most people wanted to remain with the Union. Middle Tennessee and West Tennessee wanted to secede.

However, the decision became easier after the firing on Fort Sumter. This was the beginning of the **Civil War**. Tennessee immediately seceded from the Union, and was the last state to do so.

The Civil War was fought mainly in the South and Tennessee's geographic location made it a prime target; both the Union and Confederate armies wanted to control it. The Union wanted to control Tennessee because the rivers and railroads led straight to Atlanta, Georgia, the Confederate's railroad hub. On the other hand, the Confederates needed to control Tennessee's many resources such as tobacco, cotton, livestock, iron and gunpowder.

Many battles were fought on Tennessee's soil, but none as bloody as the Battle of Shiloh. On April 6, 1862, Confederate soldiers surprised a Union unit led by **Ulysses S. Grant**, a famous general in the Union army, near the

Dred Scott

Battle of Shiloh

small Shiloh Church in Middle Tennessee and nearly defeated them. But on the second day of battle, the Union soldiers rallied together and won.

There were other famous battle sites in Tennessee. In September 1863, the Confederates once again almost defeated a Union army at Lookout Mountain near Chattanooga. The battle was fought in the mountain fog and was remembered as "The battle above the clouds". The win at the Battle of Nashville in November 1864 ultimately gave control of Tennessee to the Union.

The war brought changes for many people in Tennessee. For example, women had assumed new roles during the war, running plantations and farms, managing businesses, serving as nurses, and spying on the enemy.

Adelicia Acklen was one of the wealthiest women in Tennessee and the South. At age twenty-two, she married a wealthy cotton planter and slave trader, who was twenty-eight years her senior. After seven years of marriage, her husband died, leaving her an inheritance valued at approximately one million dollars, which included seven Louisiana cotton plantations, a two-thousand-acre farm in Middle Tennessee, and 750 slaves.

During the war, the Confederate army threatened to burn 2,800 bales of her cotton. Acklen contacted a British company and explained her situation. That company offered her one million dollars in gold if she could get it out of the South. To keep it from falling into the hands of the Confederates, Acklen secretly traveled to Louisiana and negotiated a deal with both sides to save her cotton. She managed to get a promise from the Confederates not to burn her cotton, and the Union army agreed to help her move the cotton to New Orleans. There the cotton was shipped to London and sold.

Slaves also changed roles. Many runaway slaves joined the Union army. In addition to the danger of war faced by all Civil War soldiers, black soldiers faced additional problems because of racial prejudice such as low wages, no uniforms or shoes and no health care.

Despite these obstacles, black infantrymen fought gallantly in Louisiana, Virginia and Nashville, Tennessee. It is estimated that 179,000 black men served as soldiers in the U.S. Army and another 19,000 served in the Navy. Tragically, nearly 40,000 black soldiers died over the course of the war. By the end, 16 black soldiers had been awarded the Medal of Honor for their valor.

In 1865 the Civil War came to an end. President Lincoln signed the **Emancipation Proclamation**, a document freeing all slaves. Soon after, Lincoln was tragically assassinated, leaving behind a country dealing with killed and wounded loved ones, and a broken and destroyed South. The country had to rebuild and find a new President.

Vice president **Andrew Johnson** of Tennessee had to take on the job of **Reconstruction** of the South. However, Johnson, a southerner from Tennessee, grew up during a period when most people in the South believed that slavery was necessary for the growth of the nation, and was reluctant to help free slaves. Johnson even tried to **veto** the Freedman Bureau.

The **Freedman Bureau** was a U.S. agency established during Reconstruction to help ex-slaves in their transition to freedom. This act caused Congress to mistrust Johnson and to attempt to have him **impeached**. Johnson was not removed; he finished his term quietly.

Fortunately, the **Freedman Bureau** was not vetoed and went on to help build hospitals and provide medical assistance to more than one million freed blacks. It also built more

Andrew Johnson

than 1,000 schools for black children and helped fund colleges and teacher-training institutes for blacks. The Freedman Bureau made it possible for many former slaves to further their education by going to colleges established by the bureau.

Nashville's **Fisk University** was one of those schools. In February 1862, General Clinton Bowen Fisk arrived with Union forces to emancipate slaves in Nashville. General Fisk was a compassionate man who was committed to educating former slaves. General Fisk used his influence to secure the former Union army hospital barracks to house the school.

Fisk University remains committed to its historic mission to train its students for service to humanity. Unfortunately, Congress later terminated the Freedmen Bureau.

It was time for Tennessee to get back on its feet. Progression had been waiting too long. Tennessee used its copper, coal, and iron mines to rebuild. Northerners invested in

Junior prepatory class of Fisk University, Nashville, TN

these mines, giving Tennessee the money to build larger cities and new factories that produced paper, wool and flour.

New machines such as tractors made yielding crops easier and faster. Paved roads, railroads, steamboats and bridges aided in the transportation of goods and people. In 1892, a new three-mile bridge was built over the Mississippi River from Memphis to Arkansas.

With telegraphs and telephones, people could communicate across the country in a matter of minutes that once took days. To some, the most important innovation was electricity. Electricity and the light bulb, invented by Thomas Edison, lit up the cities in Tennessee that continued to grow.

The Industrial Revolution not only brought progress; it brought problems to Tennessee. Overpopulation, factory smog and unsafe living conditions were some of the troubles the country faced. Cities were not equipped to cope with these new issues. As a result,

many cities became cesspools: health epidemics popped up all over Tennessee. Memphis suffered the hardest with four outbreaks of yellow fever. Eventually, many people left the city.

Without revenue and a low population, the city lost its **charter** in 1879. To regain its charter, people were asked to buy bonds. The first person to buy a bond was ex-slave **Robert R. Church**, who was the South's first black millionaire. His steamboat, real estate and bank investments made him one of the country's most influential men.

Church was also a philanthropist, community activist, and political leader. Church was even one of President Theodore Roosevelt's close friends. Church bought the first one thousand dollar bond to help Memphis recover after an epidemic of yellow fever. Church's financial status often took him places many people of his race could not go. This saddened Church, so he fought for civil rights for African Americans in Tennessee.

Ida B. Wells

Church was not the only Tennessean that fought for civil rights. **Ida B. Wells** was a brave black woman who wrote about unfair treatment towards people of color. Ida B. Wells was the editor of the *Memphis Free Press*, a paper that fought for equal rights for African Americans.

The Industrial Revolution revived Tennessee after the Civil War and made the state an important part of the country's economy. This renewed spirit gave Tennessee the push it needed to embark upon the twentieth century.

Terms to Know

Abraham Lincoln: the 16th President of the United States (1861-1865), who led the Union during the Civil War and emancipated slaves in the South (1863). He was assassinated shortly after the end of the war by John Wilkes Booth.

Andrew Johnson: the 17th President of the United States (1865-1869). Elected Vice President (1864), he succeeded the assassinated Abraham Lincoln as President. His administration was marked by reconstruction policies in the South and the purchase of Alaska (1867).

Civil War: a war between people in the same nation.

Confederacy: a union of persons, parties, or states; a league.

Dred Scott: American slave who sued for his liberty after spending four years with his master in a territory where slavery had been banned by the Missouri Compromise. The resulting decision by the U.S. Supreme Court (1857) declared the Missouri Compromise unconstitutional because a slave could not be taken from a master without due process of law.

Freedman Bureau: a federal agency that was formed by Congress during Reconstruction to aid distressed refugees of the American Civil War. It became primarily an agency to help the Freedmen (freed slaves) in the South.

impeach: formally accused of a wrong doing.

Industrial Revolution: the complex of radical socioeconomic changes that are brought about when extensive mechanization of production systems results in a shift from home-based hand manufacturing to large-scale factory production.

Reconstruction: the period (1865-1877) during which the states that had seceded to the Confederacy were controlled by the federal government before being readmitted to the Union.

technology: the application of science, especially to industrial or commercial objectives.

Ulysses S. Grant: the 18th President of the United States (1869-1877) and a Civil

War general. After his victorious Vicksburg campaign (1862-1863), he was made commander in chief of the Union Army (1864) and accepted the surrender of Gen. Robert E. Lee at Appomattox (1865).

Union: the United States of America regarded as a national unit, especially during the Civil War.

veto: the vested power or constitutional right of one branch or department of government to refuse approval of measures proposed by another department, especially the power of a chief executive to reject a bill passed by the legislature and thus prevent or delay its enactment into law.

Activities

1. Use a map to locate the Civil War battles fought in Tennessee.

2. Write a one-page diary entry describing the life of a Union soldier.

3. Create a timeline of technological innovations.

4. Use a Venn diagram to compare two inventions.

Want to Know More?

Web Sites

tnhistoryforkids.org/

tennesseeencyclopedia.net/

www.tennesseehistory.org/

Correlations

Performance Indicators State

6.4.spi.1.	8.4.spi.9.
6.6.spi.1.	8.4.spi.7.
7.3.spi.5.	8.4.spi.2.
7.3.spi.9.	8.5.spi.6.
7.4.spi.3.	

Correlations to McDougal Littell Textbooks

World History: Ancient Civilizations, pp. 112-117, 118-127, 128-135, 154-163, 172-181, 188-195, 226-231, 232-239, 258-265, 266-275, 304, 325-329, 370-377, 378-385, 436-441, 502-505, 514-521

World History: Medieval and Early Modern Times, pp. 46-51, 55-56, 58-65, 112-117, 118-129, 130-139, 164-173, 194-201, 222-231, 232-237, 238-243, 266-273, 298-305, 306-313, 321-325, 534-541, 542-553

World Cultures and Geography, pp. A14-A15, A18-A19, A22, A24, A26-A27, A30, A32-A33, A36, A37, 34, 35-39, 85, 109, 122, 124, 125, 126-127, 128-129, 149, 156, 157-159, 198, 199-201, 204, 205-208, 326, 327-329, 459, 460, 461-463, 496, 497-499, 535, 536, 537-539, 652, 653-654, 655, 658, 659-662, 755, 756, 757-759, 795, 796, 797-799, 824, 825-828, 851, 852, 853-854, 883, 884, 885-887, 912, 913-914, 920, 921-923

American History: Beginnings Through Reconstruction. pp. 51, 66, 68- 71, 73-75, 94, 138-140, 142, 144, 160, 163, 174, 194, 196, 198, 201, 234–241, 245–246, 250–252, 255-256, 261-269, 287, 342-344, 349, 356, 372-375, 380, 384, 395–398, 400–412, 429–438, 442, 443, 464, 493, 494, 502, 516, 518, 528, 529, 536, 540, 548, 552, 561, 582, 586, R7

The Turn of the Century

By the turn of the century, America had experienced major transformations: by World War I, thousands of immigrants lived in the United States; Hawaii and Alaska were quickly becoming a part of the U.S.; Antitrust Acts were established; the transcontinental railroad was complete and the NAACP was founded.

All of these major events affected Tennessee just as it affected the rest of the world. As a result, wealth from the industrial revolution was abundant. However, the distribution of wealth was not equal; in many cases **monopolies** were formed. For example, small Tennessee farmers could not make ends meet, while wealth created by their goods was concentrated in the hands of a few wealthy businesspeople.

Another example is the series of strikes in iron and textile industries in the 1880s. Coal miners in East Tennessee were disgruntled with insultingly low wages while owners continued to get richer.

Another injustice was the use of cheap convict labor. In 1891 and 1892, strikers freed convicts who had been leased to work for mine operators. The strikers then burned the stockades where the convicts had been housed. This uprising made national headlines and soon legislature abolished the corrupt convict lease system. Tennessee purchased state coalmines for the convicts to work in and established work facilities at a new, more humane prison at Brushy Mountain near Wartburg, Tennessee.

People began to realize that they no longer had to put up with unfair treatment. This feeling was present not only in Tennessee, but all over the world. Countries that did not have a **democracy** like the United States were experiencing civil unrest and conflict.

In 1914, WWI began with the Allied forces fighting against the Central power. The United States was neutral at first, but later joined forces with the Allies. Several hundred thousand men and women from Tennessee enlisted into the military. The state produced its share of heroes, but none more famous

Sgt. Alvin C. York

than **Alvin C. York,** a farmer from the Cumberland Mountains.

Alvin York was born in Pall Mall, Tennessee. Surprisingly, York was initially opposed to harming his fellow man and objected to war because of his religious beliefs. He was persuaded by his pastor to join the U.S. Army.

On October 8, 1918 during the Battle of the Argonne in France, York and 16 other American soldiers defeated a German machine-gun battalion. York killed about 20 German soldiers. He and the seven other surviving American soldiers captured and took 132 German prisoners.

York was promoted to sergeant as a result of his brave actions in battle. He was acknowledged as a great hero and was awarded the Distinguished Service Cross, the Congressional Medal of Honor and the French Croix de Guerre.

When he returned home, the state of Tennessee purchased a farm for him in his native Fentress County. He married his childhood sweetheart and with public donations, established the York Foundation for the education of children living in the mountains of east Tennessee.

The war sent a surge of patriotism through the United States and Tennessee. Tennesseans stepped up to help the war effort—civilians bought war bonds and women worked in factories and joined the military for the first time in history.

African Americans were also affected by the war. Workers in northern cities left factory jobs to join the military. Factories in the North promised jobs and good pay to African Americans, so thousands packed up and left the South in search of better jobs, better education, and equal treatment. This was called the **Great Migration**. Many African-Americans believed they could ecsape the racial segregation they experienced in the South by moving North.

As a result, the population in modern cities such as Chicago, New York and Detroit rapidly grew. For instance, in 1910, the African American population of Detroit was just 6,000; by 1929, this figure had risen to 120,000. The departure of hundreds of thousands of African Americans caused the black population to drop in Tennessee. Finally, in 1918, WWI ended. The Allied forces won. More than 4,000 Tennesseans had been killed or wounded in WWI.

Another transformation in Tennessee was in education. Tennessee was concerned with the deteriorating education in the state. In 1913, Governor Ben W. Hooper signed a law requiring attendance at school.

Austin Peay

Governor **Austin Peay** was also a great supporter education. In 1925, Peay established Tennessee's Department of Education.

Later that same year, Tennessee's education system became the center of national attention. A teacher named John Scopes was arrested for teaching evolution. During the

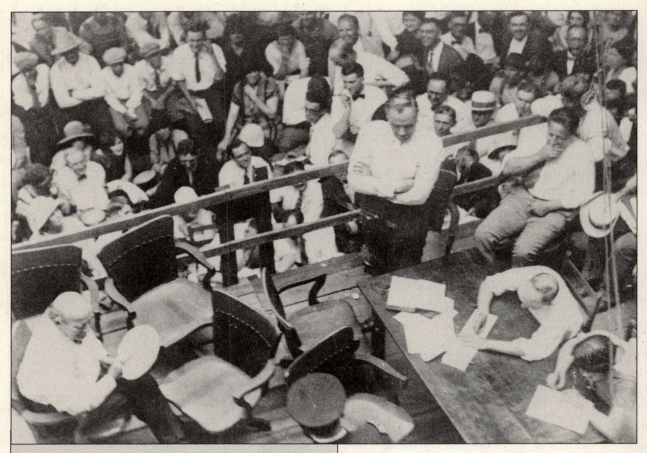

Scopes trial at an outdoor courtroom in Dayton, TN

early 1900s, many Tennesseans believed this theory to be wrong, and it was illegal to talk about anything that contradicted the Bible. So, John Scopes found himself on trail and jailed.

Also during the turn of the century, many Tennesseans experienced prosperity for the first time since before the Civil War. Women had won the right to vote and African Americans were becoming exposed to new ways of life. This sense of liberation was felt in the soul of the nation.

One expression of this liberation was through music. Blues and jazz were new American music styles. Memphis's W. C. Handy was considered to be the "Father of Blues." Handy was a composer, bandleader and publisher. He combined ragtime, Latin rhythms and the black folk music of his heritage into a unique sound known as the blues.

In 1912, Handy wrote "The Memphis Blues" on Beale Street. This song gained him national attention and established Memphis as the birthplace of the blues. Blues played a key role in the development of jazz. During the 1920s, jazz emerged as a symbol of prosperity and liberation felt by all Americans.

White America also expressed their prosperity and liberation through music. Nashville, similar to its counterpart Memphis, built a reputation as an entertainment mecca. In 1925, Nashville's *Grand Ole Opry* radio show drew thousands of listeners and dominated the barn-dance radio business. Entertainment was the focal point of the times. In fact, in 1929, the country spent four billion dollars on entertainment.

In 1929, prosperity came to a halt when the **stock market crashed**. Crashes are driven by panic as much as the economy, and usually occur after a prolonged period of rising stock prices and excessive economic optimism. This was definitely the case during the roaring twenties.

Many historians believe the crash was a major factor in **the Great Depression**. The Great Depression was a time of widespread economic despair, and Tennessee was not exempt from this disaster.

In fact, even before the Great Depression, Tennessee was lagging behind in modern innovation. Most Tennesseeans still lived on farms without electricity and indoor plumbing. Many banks, cooperations, and small businesses closed due to lack of money. Even the largest bank in Tennessee, Caldwell and Company, closed.

People lost their homes, farms and new city jobs. All over Tennessee, people had little to eat. Hungry people stood in **soup lines** established by the government to provide starving people with a piece of bread and a cup of soup.

The federal government desperately wanted to help Tennessee and other states during the Great Depression. President Franklin D. Roosevelt had a plan to help the country. This plan was called the **New Deal**. The New Deal consisted of programs designed to help unemployed people find work.

Thousands of Tennesseans were eager to take part in the programs. The New Deal had

three components: the "Three Rs." Relief was the immediate effort to help the one-third of the population most affected by the Depression. Recovery was the effort to restore normal economic health. Reform was based on the idea that the Great Depression was caused by market instability and that government intervention was necessary to balance the interests of farmers, business and labor.

These recovery programs included the Public Works Administration, the Farm Security Administration, the Work Progess Administration, the Civilan Conservation Corps, and the **Tennessee Valley Authority** (TVA).

Diagram of TVA Water Control System

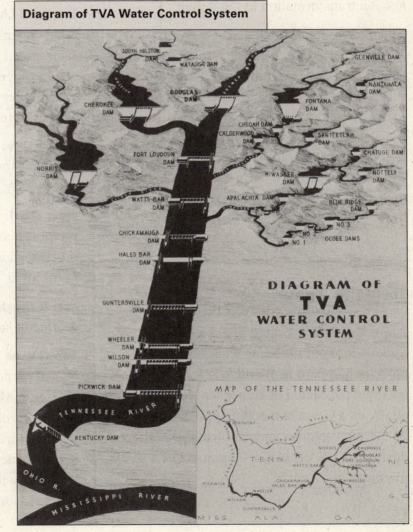

In an address to Congress on April 10, 1933, President Franklin Roosevelt asked Congress to create an agency to improve navigation, educate farmers and make the Tennessee river basin a thriving social and economic community. Congress moved swiftly, and Roosevelt signed the TVA Act on May 18, 1933, making it a part of the New Deal.

The TVA was the largest New Deal program. The Tennessee Valley Authority hired 200,000 workers to build dams in Tennessee to help control flooding and produce electricity.

In 1936, Norris Dam was the first TVA-constructed dam. The Tennessee River Basin region had suffered soil erosion that had ruined miles of farmland. The dam brought about a transformation to the region.

The most dramatic change came from TVA-generated electricity. Dams provided electricity to 60,000 Tennessee families. Electric lights and modern appliances made life easier and farms more productive. Electricity also drew industries into the region, providing desperately needed jobs. The TVA helped pull Tennessee's economy out of the Great Depression and transformed life for the better in Tennessee.

Terms to Know

Alvin C. York: a United States soldier, famous for both his being a conscientious objector and hero in World War I. He was awarded the Medal of Honor for leading an attack on a German machine gun nest, killing 25 German soldiers and capturing 132 others during the US led Meuse-Argonne Offensive in France.

Austin Peay: a native of Kentucky, Austin Peay came to Clarksville, Tennessee and opened a law practice in 1896. He was first elected to the Tennessee House of Representatives in 1901 and re-elected in 1903. A strong supporter of public education, Peay obtained the Democratic Party nomination for governor in 1922 to oppose incumbent Republican governor Alfred A. Taylor.

democracy: government by the people, exercised either directly or through elected representatives.

evolution: a theory that humans developed from apes.

Great Migration: the movement of over a million African Americans out of the rural Southern United States from 1914 to 1950. African Americans migrated to escape the widespread racism of the South, to seek out employment opportunities in urban environments, and to pursue what was widely perceived to be a "better life" in the North.

monopoly: exclusive control by one group of the means of producing or selling a commodity or service.

New Deal: the programs and policies to promote economic recovery and social reform introduced during the 1930s by President Franklin D. Roosevelt.

stock market crash: a sudden dramatic decline of stock prices.

Tennessee Valley Authority: a federally owned corporation created by congressional charter in May 1933 to provide navigation, flood control, electricity generation, fertilizer manufacturing, and economic development in the Tennessee Valley, a region particularly hard hit by the Great Depression. The TVA was envisioned not only as an electricity provider, but also as a regional economic development agency that would use federal experts and electricity to rapidly modernize the region's economy and society.

The Great Depression: the beginning of the Great Depression in the United States is associated with the stock market crash on October 29, 1929, known as Black Tuesday. International trade declined sharply, as did personal incomes, tax revenues, prices and profits. Cities all around the world were hit hard, especially those dependent on heavy industry.

Activities

1. Write a letter to a Southern family describing life after migration to the North.

2. Create a song that expresses life at the turn of 21st century. Use a chart to compare that song with a song written at the turn of the 20th century.

3. Write a commentary on what Austin Peay would think of education in Tennessee today.

4. Have groups of students debate for or against a monopoly. Use Bill Gates' Microsoft and John D. Rockefeller's Standard Oil Company as examples.

Want to Know More?

Web Sites

tnhistoryforkids.org/

tennesseeencyclopedia.net/

www.tennesseehistory.org/

Correlations

Performance Indicators State

6.1.spi.8.	7.3.spi.4.
6.4.spi.1.	7.4.spi.1.
6.5.spi.5.	7.5.spi.1.
6.6.spi.1.	8.2.spi.10.
7.2.spi.5.	8.3.spi.3.
7.3.spi.3.	8.5.spi.6.

Correlations to McDougal Littell Textbooks

World History: Ancient Civilizations, pp. 53, 59-62, 84-85, 104-105, 112-117, 118-135, 154-163, 172-181, 188-200, 206-207, 224-239, 258-275, 277-280, 304, 325-329, 350-351, 370-385, 405-409, 436-441, 502-505, 514-521

World History: Medieval and Early Modern Times, pp. 46-51, 55-56, 58-65, 69, 72, 112-117, 118-129, 130-139, 156-161, 164-173, 180-184, 194-201, 222-231, 232-237, 238-243, 266-273, 298-305, 306-313, 321-325, 326-331, 402, 414-415, 442-443, 444-450, 497-501, 503-507, 512, 520-526, 534-541, 542-553

World Cultures and Geography, pp. A19, 58, 63, 69, 79-81, 109, 147-149, 177-178, 180, 234-235, 247, 264, 293-295, 336, 337, 344, 353, 373, 402-404, 410, 415-417, 427, 439, 488, 502-503, 509, 572, 587, 591, 599, 610, 627, 628, 635, 678, 680, 709-710, 717-718, 765-766, 770, 778-779, 781-783, 785-786, 814, 816, 828, 836-839, 841-842, 861, 862, 894, 895, 903

American History: Beginnings Through Reconstruction, pp. 4–11, 51, 62–64, 66, 79, 80, 81, 94–96, 98, 103–104, 107, 108–109, 111–112, 134–135, 142, 144, 160, 163, 174, 194, 196, 198, 201, 343, 344, 349, 356, 372, 374, 375, 381, 402, 407, 438, 442, 443, 464, 516, 518, 528, 529, 536, 540, 548, 552, 561, 582, 586, R7

Major Events of the 20th Century

For many people, the two most memorable events that took place during the twentieth century were WWII and the Civil Rights Movement.

World War II was a conflict that involved virtually every part of the world between 1939 and 1945. There were two sides in the conflict: Germany, Japan, and Italy were called the Axis Powers. The Allies included the United States, Great Britain, France, the Soviet Union, and China.

Most people know the Allies were victorious, but most people do not know the major role Tennessee played in that victory.

While World War II raged across Europe between 1939 and 1941, the United States tried to remain neutral, but cautious. Instead of being unprepared for war, the U.S. quickly converted the sluggish economy of the Depression into a defense production industry.

In further preparation for the possibility of war, the U.S. Congress enacted its first peacetime draft, the Selective Service and Training Act. Tennessee reacted by establishing the state's first defense organization, the **Advisory Committee on Preparedness**.

In 1941, Tennessee legislature created a Tennessee State Guard, the largest in the South. Also in 1941, the state bought and cleared over three thousand acres in Middle Tennessee to lease to the federal government. In June of that year, Major General George S. Patton conducted armored maneuvers in that area.

Despite preparations for the war, the state and the nation were stunned to hear the news of Japan's attack on **Pearl Harbor** on December 7, 1941. This day would be imprinted on American memories forever.

USS Shaw explodes during the Japanese raid on Pearl Harbor, December 7, 1941

Tennesseans quickly joined branches of the armed forces. True to the nickname of the "Volunteer State," Tennesseans supported the war not only through the armed services, but also in their home front activities: they purchased rationed food, collected scrap metals, and saved kitchen fats, which were used in the production of glycerin for bombs.

Second atomic bombing of Nagasaki, Japan, August 1945

Churches, YMCAs, YWCAs, and other groups opened canteens for the soldiers, and invested in war bonds. In addition, Tennessee became the site of numerous military installations, training facilities, and prisoner of war camps.

As it became increasingly clear that the war would not end quickly, **President Franklin D. Roosevelt** felt it was time for a decisive move, with Tennessee playing a leading role. In 1939, **Albert Einstein** sent a letter warning President Roosevelt of the possibility that **Adolph Hitler's** Nazi Germany could construct a revolutionary weapon capable of creating mass destruction.

After Pearl Harbor was attacked, America urgently began constructing an **atomic bomb**. The construction of such a weapon required vital components: land, electricity and clean water. East Tennessee was selected to provide these resources that could construct an atomic bomb before the Germans could do it.

In September 1942, the **Manhattan Project** began. The project required vast amounts of electricity, which the Tennessee Valley Authority could provide. There was an abundance of clean water in East Tennessee,

and the land could be acquired cheaply. Since the project needed thousands of employees, a city for the workers on the Manhattan Project was established, called Oak Ridge.

After the war, the world was horrified by the devastation. Countries were inspired to come together and work toward peace. Each country needed a representative to discuss the steps to achieve that goal—**Cordell Hull** was chosen to represent the United States.

Cordell Hull

Cordell Hull was born on October 2, 1871, in a small log cabin in the mountains of upper middle Tennessee. Hull attended Cumberland University were he received his law degree. He practiced law and soon became interested in politics, serving in many capacities of the government.

In 1933, President Franklin D. Roosevelt appointed Hull to be secretary of state for his loyal service. In that office, Hull did much to forge defense treaties between the United States and other counties. During World War II he represented the U.S. in the establishment of the United Nations.

The United Nations was created after WWII ended to maintain world peace, develop good relations between countries, promote cooperation in solving the world's problems, and encourage respect for human rights. In 1944, Hull was appointed senior adviser to the United States delegation of the United Nations Conference on International Organization, and was awarded the 1945 Nobel Peace Prize. In Tennessee, Cordell Hull is considered the Father of the United Nations.

Perhaps the single most important influence WWII had on Tennessee was its impact on the state's economy. The growth of the war industry in Tennessee brought the state out of the Depression.

The war also provided a catalyst for the employment of large numbers of women and African Americans. Women worked in textile, chemical, iron, steel, aircraft and aluminum factories, as well as in communications and government agencies.

During the war many African Americans moved from rural farm areas to war production centers in Tennessee. The war industries generally paid three times as much as domestic work. World War II had touched nearly all the lives in Tennessee by drastically reshaping the economy and changing views of the world for years to come.

Segregation

During Reconstruction, African Americans in Tennessee experienced a brief encounter with equality. Tennessee elected African American congressmen, and the Freedmen Bureau assisted African Americans with establishing businesses, attending college and purchasing land. Unfortunately, that utopia did not last long.

Near the end of the nineteenth century, racial attitudes in Tennessee and the country hardened. Laws were put in place to control many aspects of the African American community.

In 1896, the U.S. Supreme Court gave legal sanction to **segregation** in the historic *Plessy* v *Ferguson* decision that established the principle of "separate but equal." For nearly sixty years, people in Tennessee and the United States lived in a separate but not–so–equal society.

In 1945, WWII came to an end. To the rest of the world, many African Americans were considered heroes, but at home they were treated as second-class citizens. African Americans had fought and sacrificed their lives for a country that was a participant in a war that freed oppressed people. This was an enormous contradiction. However, they had a new spirit. This spirit urged African Americans in Tennessee to wage a war against racial oppression. This was the start of the **Civil Rights Movement**.

Martin Luther King, Jr.

Dr. Martin Luther King, Jr., Thurgood Marshall, Rosa Parks, and the NAACP, among others, began to strive for equality. Through marches and legal victories such as the **Montgomery Bus Boycott** and *Brown v Board of Education*, African Americans witnessed some change.

The most profound change was the **Civil Rights Act of 1964**. The Act outlawed segregation in U.S. schools and public places. Unfortunately, there were still battles to be fought. One in particular was the Memphis Sanitation Workers Strike of 1968.

Most people believe the biggest mistake Memphis ever made was not settling the Sanitation Strike sooner. The Sanitation Strike in Memphis is one of the most famous strikes in Tennessee history. For years, there had been unrest among the African American sanitation workers because of the unfair conditions they had to endure. For example, African American workers were often sent home without pay or worked off the clock while white workers in the same department continued to work and be paid.

Conditions got worse. In February of 1968, two African American sanitation workers were crushed to death by a malfunctioning garbage truck. They had been inside the truck to escape the rain long enough to eat their lunch. Both of the dead men were new to the job and did not have life insurance policies. This caused an uproar among the African American workmen. The Memphis Sanitation Workers Strike began on February 12, 1968.

Dr. Martin Luther King, Jr. came to Memphis to speak to the striking workers. A march was planned to support the strike, but the first attempt failed due to an unruly crowd. One young marcher was even shot and killed by the police. This was disconcerting to Dr. King. He felt strongly about leading a peaceful march in Memphis; it had been accomplished in other cities. Dr. Martin Luther King, Jr. and his associates arrived in Memphis to lead a peaceful march scheduled for April 8th.

On the night of April 3, 1968, at Mason Temple, Dr. King foretold of his own death to the congregation in the "Mountain Top" speech. At the time it seemed prophetic. In retrospect, it was sadly inevitable. Dr. King told the crowd that he was not afraid to die and that he was grateful to God for allowing him a vision of the promise land for his people.

Later that evening, Dr. King and his entourage prepared to leave to have dinner with Memphis pastor Billy Kyles. At 6:00 p.m., while walking down the steps of the Lorraine Motel, Dr, King was shot. Dr. King's friends delivered him to St. Joseph's Hospital within 15 minutes.

The doctors performed emergency surgery, but the wound was too serious. Dr. Martin Luther King, Jr. was pronounced dead at 7:05 p.m. He was 39 years old. Memphis was soon flooded with Federal officials including the Attorney General of the United States. It was soon announced James Earl Ray was the killer.

The **assassination** caused widespread grief. Violent outrage spewed out of Memphis and many other cities. Tennessee, along with the country, witnessed chaotic riots that caused enormous damage.

President Lyndon Johnson used his influence to make the Memphis City Government come to an agreement with the sanitation workers. A special interrogation committee stated that Ray was guilty, but did not act alone. Ray never implicated anyone else, and took his secrets to the grave.

Terms to Know

Albert Einstein: German-born American theoretical physicist whose special and general theories of relativity revolutionized modern thought on the nature of space and time and formed a theoretical base for the exploitation of atomic energy. He won a 1921 Nobel Prize for his explanation of the photoelectric effect.

assassination: to murder (a prominent person) by surprise attack for political reasons.

atomic bomb: a bomb deriving its destructive power from the release of nuclear energy.

Brown v Board of Education: a landmark decision of the United States Supreme Court which declared that state laws which established separate public schools for black and white students denied black children equal educational opportunities.

Civil Rights Act of 1964: landmark legislation in the United States that outlawed segregation in U.S. schools and public places. First conceived to help African Americans, the bill was amended to protect women in courts, and explicitly included white people for the first time. It also started the Equal Employment Opportunity Commission.

Cordell Hull: American public official who as secretary of state (1933-1944) laid the groundwork for the founding of the United Nations. He was awarded the 1945 Nobel Peace Prize.

Dr. Martin Luther King, Jr.: American cleric whose eloquence and commitment to nonviolent tactics formed the foundation of the civil rights movement of the 1950s and 1960s.. He won the 1964 Nobel Peace Prize, four years before he was assassinated in Memphis, Tennessee.

Manhattan Project: the project to develop the first nuclear weapon (atomic bomb) during World War II by the United States, the United Kingdom and Canada.

Montgomery Bus Boycott: a political and social protest campaign started in 1955 in

Montgomery, Alabama, intended to oppose the city's policy of racial segregation on its public transit system. The struggle lasted from December 5, 1955, to December 20, 1956, and led to a United States Supreme Court decision that declared the Alabama and Montgomery laws requiring segregated buses unconstitutional.

NAACP: the National Association for the Advancement of Colored People is one of the oldest and most influential radical civil rights organizations in the United States.

Pearl Harbor: an inlet of the Pacific Ocean on the southern coast of Oahu, Hawaii. It became the site of a naval base after the United States annexed Hawaii in 1900. On Sunday, December 7, 1941, Japanese planes attacked the base, and the United States entered World War II the following day.

President Franklin D. Roosevelt: the 32nd President of the United States (1933-1945). Governor of New York (1929-1932), he ran for President with the promise of a New Deal for the American people. His administration was marked by relief programs, measures to increase employment and assist industrial and agricultural recovery from the Depression, and World War II. He was the only U.S. President to be reelected three times (1936, 1940, and 1944). He died in office.

segregation: the policy or practice of separating people of different races, classes, or ethnic groups, as in schools, housing, and public or commercial facilities, especially as a form of discrimination.

Activities

1. Have a class debate on strikes. Is striking an effective means to obtain results?

2. Create a biography mobile, with brief biographies and pictures of Civil Rights leaders.

3. Compare WWII with the current Iraq war using a Venn diagram.

4. Using a map of Tennessee, locate dams built for the TVA.

Want to Know More?

Web Sites

tnhistoryforkids.org/

tennesseeencyclopedia.net/

www.tennesseehistory.org/

Correlations

Performance Indicators State

6.1.spi.8.	7.3.spi.4.
6.3.spi.6.	7.4.spi.1.
6.4.spi.1.	7.5.spi.1.
6.5.spi.5.	8.2.spi.10.
6.6.spi.1.	8.3.spi.3.
7.2.spi.5.	8.5.spi.6.
7.3.spi.3.	

Correlations to McDougal Littell Textbooks

World History: Ancient Civilizations, pp. 53, 59-62, 84-85, 104-105, 112-117, 118-127, 128-135, 154-163, 172-181, 188-200, 206-207, 224-225, 226-231, 232-239, 258-265, 266-275, 277-280, 304, 325-329, 350-351, 370-377, 378-385, 405-409, 436-441, 487, 502-505, 514-521, R13

World History: Medieval and Early Modern Times, pp. 46-51, 55-56, 58-65, 69, 72, 112-117, 118-129, 130-139, 156-161, 164-173, 180-184, 194-201, 222-231, 232-237, 238-243, 266-273,

298-305, 306-313, 321-325, 326-331, 402, 414-415, 442-443, 444-450, 497-501, 503-507, 512, 534-541, 542-553, S16, 520-526, R13

World Cultures and Geography, pp. A19, 58, 63, 69, 79-81, 109, 147-149, 177-178, 180, 234-235, 247, 264, 293-295, 336, 337, 344, 353, 373, 402-404, 410, 415-417, 427, 439, 488, 502-503, 509, 572, 587, 591, 599, 610, 627, 628, 635, 678, 680, 709-710, 717-718, 765-766, 770, 778-779, 781, 782-783, 785-786, 814, 816, 828, 836-837, 838-839, 841-842, 861, 862, 894, 895, 903

American History: Beginnings Through Reconstruction, pp. 4–11, 51, 62-64, 66, 79-81, 94-96, 98, 103–104, 107, 108–109, 111–112, 134–135, 142, 144, 160, 163, 174, 194, 196, 198, 201, 343, 344, 349, 356, 372, 374, 375, 381, 402, 407, 438, 442, 443, 464, 516, 518, 528, 529, 536, 540, 548, 552, 561, 582, 586, R7

Tennessee's Government

Archaeologists' studies of prehistoric sites reveal that chieftains probably led bands of Ice Age hunters into the Tennessee area about ten thousand years ago.

The Old Stone Fort in Coffee County, Tennessee is an earthen structure built by Woodland people around 30 A.D. There is evidence of a system of rules and laws and the presence of leadership by a chief or king.

Later, European explorers found that Native Americans were not uncivilized but had a rather advanced political system. Cherokees, Creeks, and Chickasaws established patriarchal systems of government centered on chiefs, sub-chiefs, and councils of advisors.

The Cherokees were a patriarchal society, although women held powerful positions and helped make important decisions. Creeks had elders called "beloved men," who dealt with matters of war and peace and ceremonies.

Cherokees, Creeks, Chickasaws, Choctaws, and Shawnees all utilized a clan system of family. A **clan** is group of families related through a common ancestor or marriage. This insured a foundation built on relationships interwoven with political and religious elements of life.

By the mid-1600s, British settlers came under the rule of the British monarchy. A **monarchy** is a society ruled by one person, such as a king. By the late 1770s there were 13 British colonies in North America. Of those 13 colonies, North Carolina claimed the Tennessee frontier.

One of the first settlements in Tennessee was Watauga, located far away from the other colonies. It took weeks for help, news or food to reach Watauga. In 1772, the settlers in Watauga, feeling isolated from the other colonies, decided to develop the Watauga Association. They created a system of laws and organized a government. They called their system of laws the **Watauga Compact**.

Many people believe the Watauga Compact was the first constitution in North America. Eight years later, pioneers at the French Lick on the Cumberland River drew up the **Cumberland Compact** for similar purposes. Neither compact survived.

The settlers had had enough of a monarchy. In 1775, the 13 colonies went to war against Britain. This war became known as the American Revolution. The Americans won the war—therefore, a new set of rules was needed. The United States Constitution was formed.

In 1784, North Carolina gave control of its Tennessee lands to the United States government. When Tennessee settlers received this news they tried to form their own government. They named it Franklin after Benjamin Franklin.

Franklin failed because of lack of support from the government and excessive meddling from North Carolina. Nevertheless, settlers continued to move into the Tennessee territory.

By 1795, Tennessee's population had over 75,000 people—enough to officially form a state. On June 1, 1796, President George Washington signed legislation, admitting Tennessee as the sixteenth state in the Union. Tennesseans elected John Sevier as their first governor.

The Tennessee government mirrors the United States government: both believe in democracy. A **democracy** is a form of government in which the people take part. The citizens help make decisions for the common good. No one person or group has total power. It also protects the rights of the citizens.

Both governments have a **constitution,** which is a written statement outlining the basic laws or principles by which a country is governed. Tennessee's first constitution was written in 1796. On May 19, 1834, Tennessee revised their constitution. The revisions addressed farmer's rights, eliminated property requirements for voting, and the election of fixed termed officials.

However, freed African Americans, who had voted under the 1796 Constitution, lost the right to vote in this constitution. After the Civil War, Tennessee had a lot of restructuring, and began revising their constitution again. On March 26, 1870, the constitution was **ratified,** or approved. In this revision, slavery was abolished and African American men regained their right to vote. The third constitution is still followed today in Tennessee.

Tennessee's constitution outlines the state's government, and the United States Constitution explains how our national government is to be run. Our national government has three branches: executive, judicial and legislature. Each branch has its own set of responsibilities. The legislature makes the laws, the judicial explains and applies the laws, and the executive enforces the laws.

Just like the United States, Tennessee developed three branches. Under the Tennessee constitution, **legislative** authority of the state is vested in the General Assembly,

which consists of a Senate and a House of Representatives, both dependent upon the people to be elected. The name of the legislative authority may vary from state to state, but the official title in Tennessee is the "General Assembly of the State of Tennessee," but may also be properly referred to as the legislature. The General Assembly has 33 Senators and 99 representatives.

The **judicial branch** is made up of courts and judges. Voters elect judges to eight-year terms for the state court.

The Tennessee Supreme Court is the state's highest court. It normally meets in Jackson, Knoxville, and Nashville, as required by the state constitution. The five justices may accept appeals of civil and criminal cases from lower state courts. They also interpret the laws and constitutions of Tennessee and the United States.

The Supreme Court may assume jurisdiction over undecided cases in the Court of Appeals or Court of Criminal Appeals when there is special need for a speedy decision. The court also has appellate jurisdiction in cases involving state taxes, the right to hold public office, and issues of constitutional law.

Nashville and the Cumberland River

The **executive branch** carries out the state laws. The governor is the leader of Tennessee's executive branch. He **appoints** 21 people to serve in the governor's **cabinet**. The cabinet is in charge of state programs such as the department of education.

Throughout the state's rich political heritage, Tennesseans have played important roles in shaping the character of our nation's government. Three presidents, a secretary of state, United States House of Representatives, and many others have served on the federal level.

Today, Tennesseans remain influential in all levels of the federal government. Members of Congress hold vital roles for Tennesseans in the federal government. Members of Congress are not only responsible for making federal law and overseeing the administration of the U.S. Government, but they are heavily involved in assisting citizens in dealing with federal agencies as well.

Congressmen spend most of their time handling constituents' or citizens' requests. As a result, each branch and position is separate and functions on a system of checks and balances. Checks and balances is the ability of each branch of the government to exercise or controls, over the other branches. This protects the rights of all Tennesseans, which is why the forefathers wrote the constitution.

Tennessee's Governors

John Sevier, 1796–1801; 1803–1809, Democrat

Willie Blount, 1809–1815, Democrat

Sam Houston, 1827–1829, Democrat

William Hall, April–October 1829, Democrat

Newton Cannon, 1835–1839, Whig

James Knox Polk, 1839–1841, Democrat

James Chamberlain Jones, 1841–1845, Whig

Aaron Venable Brown, 1845–1847, Democrat

Neill Smith Brown, 1847–1849, Whig

William Trousdale, 1849–1851, Democrat

William Bowen Campbell, 1851–1853, Whig

Andrew Johnson, 1853–1857 (civil); 1862–1865 (Military), Democrat

Isham Green Harris, 1857–1862, Democrat

Robert Looney Caruthers, 1863, Democrat

William Gannaway Brownlow, 1865–1869, Whig

Dewitt Clinton Senter, 1869–1871, Whig/Republican

James Davis Porter, 1875–1879, Democrat

John Calvin Brown, 1871–1875, Whig/Democrat

Albert Smith Marks, 1879–1881, Democrat

Alvin Hawkins, 1881–1883, Whig/Republican

William Brimage Bate, 1883–1887, Democrat

Robert Love Taylor, 1887–1891; 1897–1899, Democrat

John Price Buchanan, 1891–1893, Farm-Labor

Peter Turney, 1893–1897, Democrat

Benton McMillin, 1899–1903, Democrat

James Beriah Frazier, 1903–1905, Democrat

John Isaac Cox, 1905–1907, Democrat

Malcolm Rice Patterson, 1907–1911, Democrat

Ben Walter Hooper, 1911–1915, Republican

Thomas Clarke Rye, 1915–1919, Democrat

Albert Houston Roberts, 1919–1921, Democrat

Alfred Alexander Taylor, 1921–1923, Republican

Austin Peay, 1923–1927, Democrat

Henry Hollis Horton, 1927–1933, Democrat

Hill McAlister, 1933–1937, Democrat

Gordon Weaver Browning, 1937–1939; 1949–1953, Democrat

William Prentice Cooper, 1939–1945, Democrat

Jim Nance McCord, 1945–1949, Democrat

Frank Goad Clement, 1953–1959; 1963–1967, Democrat

Earl Buford Ellington, 1959–1963; 1967–1971, Democrat

Bryant Winfield Culberson Dunn, 1971–1975, Republican

Leonard Ray Blanton, 1975–1979, Democrat

Andrew Lamar Alexander, 1979–1987, Republican

Ned Ray McWherter, 1987–1995, Democrat

Donald Kenneth Sundquist, 1996–2003, Republican

Tennessee's current Governor: Phil Bredesen

Terms to Know

appoint: to select or designate to fill an office or a position.

cabinet: a body of persons appointed by a head of state or a prime minister to head the executive departments of the government and to act as official advisers.

clan: a division of a tribe tracing descent from a common ancestor.

constitution: the system of fundamental laws and principles that prescribes the nature, functions, and limits of a government or another institution.

democracy: government by the people, exercised either directly or through elected representatives.

executive: the branch of government charged with putting into effect a country's laws and the administering of its functions.

judicial: of, relating to, or proper to courts of law or to the administration of justice.

legislative: having the power to create laws; intended to legislate.

monarchy: a society ruled by a sole and absolute ruler.

ratify: to approve and give formal sanction to; confirm.

Activity

Write your own constitution! Describe what issues and laws are most important to you in your life and share it with your classmates.

Want to Know More?

Web Sites

tnhistoryforkids.org/

tennesseeencyclopedia.net/

www.tennesseehistory.org/

Correlations

Performance Indicators State

6.4.spi.1.	8.4.spi.2.
6.4.spi.4.	8.4.spi.3.
7.4.spi.1.	8.4.spi.4.
8.4.spi.1.	8.4.spi.5.

Correlations to McDougal Littell Textbooks

World History: Ancient Civilizations, pp. 99-100, 112-117, 118-127, 128-135, 154-163, 172-181, 188-195, 226-231, 232-239, 258-265, 266-275, 308-309, 370-377, 378-385, 436-441, 514-521

World History: Medieval and Early Modern Times, pp. 46-51, 58-65, 112-117, 118-129, 130-139, 151, 164-173, 194-201, 222-231, 232-237, 238-243, 266-273, 295-305, 306-313, 534-541, 542-553

World Cultures and Geography, pp. 79-81, 147-148, 177-178, 234-235, 264, 293, 336, 337, 344, 402-403, 415-417, 587, 591, 628, 635, 678, 680, 717-718, 765-766, 770, 785-786, 814, 816, 841-842, 861, 862, 894, 895, 903

American History: Beginnings Through Reconstruction, pp. 8, 15, 17–18, 27, 30–33, 36–37, 46, 64-65, 68, 69, 71, 73-75, 96–97, 138-140, 144, 156–188, 196, 197, 205–207, 224–228, 234–256, 261–299, 300–303, 318–325, 328–332, 338–343, 346, 352–358, 379, 381–386, 397–401, 404–406, 428–437, 483–486, 500–503, 511, 538–540, 543, 544, 561- 564, 570–575, 583- 586, 588

Interesting Facts about Tennessee

- Tennessee's nickname "The Volunteer State" originated during the War of 1812 when thousands of Tennesseans enlisted in response to Governor Blount's call for volunteers.

- Tennessee's capitol city is Nashville, located in Davidson County. Tennessee's largest city is Memphis with a population of 650,100 in 2000.

Memphis

- The National Civil Rights Museum is located at the Lorraine Motel, the site of Dr. Martin Luther King's assassination in Memphis, Tennessee.

- Knoxville, Tennessee is home to the Women's Basketball Hall of Fame.

- The U. S. Congress recognized Bristol as the birth place of country music in 1998 for its contributions to early country music recordings and ongoing influence.

Presidents from Tennessee

- Andrew Jackson, 7th President, 1829–1837

- James K. Polk, 11th President, 1845–1849

- Andrew Johnson, 17th President, 1865–1869

Al Gore

- Albert Gore, Jr., 45th Vice President, 1993–2001

Arts and Music

- Graceland, the home of rock-and-roll pioneer Elvis Presley, is located in Memphis, Tennessee.

- Since 1925, a live country music show has been performed every weekend at Grand Ole Opry in Nashville.

- Dolly Parton, a famous country-western singer, founded Dollywood, a family entertainment park, in Pigeon Forge near the Great Smoky Mountains National Park.

- The Beale Street Historic District is considered the birthplace of blues music. Bessie Smith and W.C. Handy both performed there.

- Alex Haley won the Pulitzer Prize for his

legendary book, *Roots: The Saga of an American Family.*

- Frances Hodgson Burnett wrote over 40 books. Her most famous, *The Secret Garden* and *The Little Princess* were made into movies.

- Knoxville native James Agee was nominated for an Academy Award for the film *The African Queen.*

- Famous poet Nikki Giovanni grew up in Tennessee.

- Film director and screenplay writer Craig Brewer grew up in Tennessee. His famous movie *Hustle & Flow,* filmed in Memphis, won at the 2005 Sundance Film Festival. The rap group Three Six Mafia won the Academy Award for Best Original Song.

- Kathleen Bates, an Academy Award winning actress, was born in Memphis.

- Memphis native Justin Timberlake has won four Grammys and one Emmy award.

- Other artists from Tennessee: Dixie Carter, Tina Tunner, Cybil Shepard, Annie Potts, Patricia Neal, Samuel L. Jackson, Isaac Hayes, George Hamilton, Morgan Freeman, Aretha Franklin, Billy Ray Cyrus, Johnny Cash and Pat Boone.

Sports

- Wilma Rudolph overcame sickness and racial prejudice to become a four time, three gold, Olympic games winner.

- Anfernee "Penny" Hardaway, born in Memphis, has become a famous NBA player.

- Sterling Martin was born in Columbus, Tennessee, and is a two-time Daytona 500 winner.

Wilma Rudolph at the finish line

- Football star Peyton Manning attended The University of Tennessee from 1994 to 1997.

- The Tennessee Titans are a professional American Football team based in Nashville, Tennessee.

- The Memphis Grizzlies are professional basketball team located in Memphis.

Entrepreneurs

- The company Fed Ex was founded in Memphis, Tennessee in 1973 by Fred Smith.

- David Lynskey is the creator and founder of the International Titanium Bicycles company.

- Earl Bentz from Ashland City, Tennessee, is the owner and creator of Triton Boats.

Maps and Symbols

Tennessee Highway Map

Tennessee Rivers Map

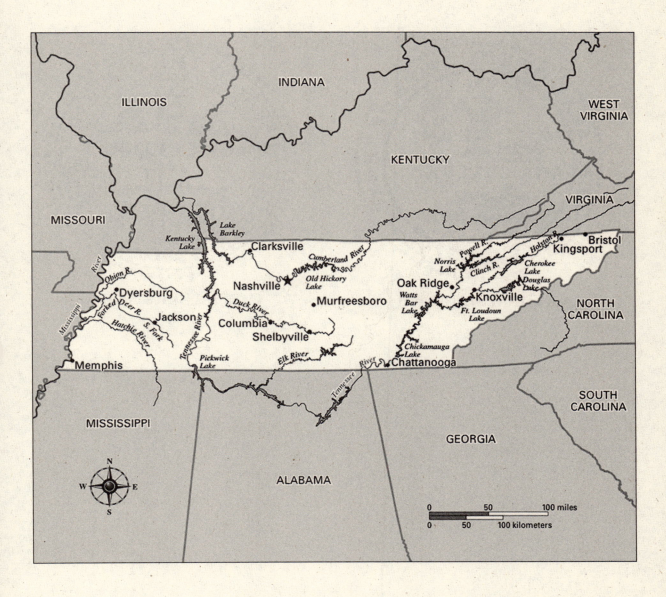

Original State Seal

Official State Seal

Mockingbird, State Bird

Tennessee State Flag

Iris, State Flower